US CITIZENSHIP
TEST STUDY GUIDE
2025

WHAT YOU NEED TO FACE
THE NATURALIZATION
EXAM FREE FROM
DOUBT

ALL THE 100 USCIS QUESTIONS WITH COMPREHENSIVE ANSWERS EXPLANATIONS

CLEAR AND CONCISE REVIEW CHAPTERS

14 PRACTICE TESTS:
8 FOR CIVICS
2 FOR READING
2 FOR WRITING
2 FOR SPEAKING

INCLUDES COMPREHENSIVE REVIEW FOR ALL 100 USCIS CIVICS QUESTIONS

Bonus Flashcards

Dear student, thank you for the trust you are giving us by choosing our "U.S. Citizenship Study Guide".

Go to page 50 to receive your 100 printable bonus Flashcards now.

TABLE OF CONTENTS

Introduction to the U.S. Naturalization/ Citizenship Test

The United States Citizenship and Immigration Services (USCIS) conducts the naturalization test to ensure that the person applying is eligible and meets all the requirements to become a U.S. citizen. Before the actual test (also called the "Interview"), USCIS conducts an investigation of the applicant's background to check that he meets the requirements listed in the next chapter.

Once it is determined that the candidate meets the requirements, he is called for the naturalization exam, also known as the Interview. During the Interview, a USCIS officer verifies the applicant's English proficiency by asking questions about his background and asking him to read and write a few simple sentences. This part of the exam is called the "English test."

Finally, the USCIS officer asks the candidate additional questions to verify that he has basic knowledge regarding American history, American government, and civics. This second part of the exam is called "civics test."

This guide will brief you on the requirements, process, and learning material to pass your naturalization exam.

Eligibility and Requirements for Applying for the U.S. Naturalization/ Citizenship Test

Eligibility Factors

Eligibility mainly depends on the following factors:

- Green Card duration and special circumstances

- Military service

- Duration of physical stay in the U.S.

Eligibility Conditions

- If you are a Green Card holder and have lived in the U.S. for at least 30 months (2.5 years), you are eligible to apply for naturalization after 5 years of obtaining your Green Card.

- If you are a Green Card holder and married to a U.S. citizen, and you have lived in the U.S. for a minimum of 18 months (1.5 years), you are eligible to apply for naturalization after 3 years of obtaining your Green Card.

- If you are NOT a Green Card holder, but have served in the U.S. military for at least 1 year in peacetime, you can apply for naturalization while on active duty or within six months of honorable separation from the military service.

- If you are a widow/widower of a U.S. citizen who lost their life while serving in the military, you are eligible to apply for naturalization without a Green Card or physical residence conditions.

- If you are a Green Card holder and have less than 1 year of peacetime military service, physically living in the U.S. for at least 30 months (2.5 years) makes you eligible to apply for naturalization after 5 years of obtaining your Green Card.

- If you are a Green Card holder with at least 1 year of military service who has been honorably discharged from service more than 6 months before, a living experience of 30 months (2.5 years) makes you eligible to apply for naturalization after 5 years of obtaining your Green Card.

- If you have served in the military during wartime, you are eligible to apply for Naturalization at any time without the condition of physical living and/or the possession of a Green Card.

Eligibility Requirements

The above eligibility criteria must also meet the following requirements to be eligible for the process of becoming a U.S. citizen through naturalization.

- Your minimum age should be 18 years or above.

- "Good moral character" is a must requirement. In simple terms, you must not have indulged in any criminal or unlawful activity during your lifetime. If you are found lying during or after your naturalization interview about your criminal record, it will lead to the immediate cancellation of your naturalization process, and you will become ineligible in the future.

- In the U.S. state where you plan to become a resident, you must have stayed there for a minimum of three months.

- During your wait period of 3 or 5 years (depending upon conditions), you cannot take trips outside of the U.S. for six months or more.

- A two-part naturalization test – an English-language test (to be discussed in detail in the sections below, mainly consists of language proficiency in reading, writing, and speaking), and a civics test (it will also be discussed later, this section consists of basic knowledge of U.S. history and government).

- If you are a male and have lived in the U.S. while between the ages of 18-25, you must voluntarily register with the Selective Service System.

- You must volunteer to serve in U.S. military service or do civil service when you are asked.

Exceptions for Disabled and Seniors

- A Green Card holder whose age is 50 or above and who has lived in the U.S. for at least 20 years is exempt from the "English language requirement". Therefore, the candidate will not have to take the English test and can take the civics test in his or her native language.

- A Green Card holder aged 55 or above who has lived in the U.S. for at least 15 years is exempt from the "English language requirement". Therefore, the candidate will not have to take the English test and can take the civics test in his or her native language.

- A Green Card holder aged 65 or above who has lived in the U.S. for at least 20 years is exempt from the "English language requirement". Therefore, the candidate will not have to take the English test and can take the civics test in his or her native language. Moreover, in the civics test, the candidate is required to study only 20 of the mandatory 100 questions. Within the chapter on the 100 USCIS civics test questions in this guide, the 20 questions for people over 65 who lived in the U.S. for at least 20 years are highlighted with an asterisk (*).

- Medical disability-related applicants who have lived in or are planning to live in the U.S. for at least 1 year are not required to take both civics and English tests. However, they will be required to produce medical certifications for the exemption of either or both.

Failing English or Civics Tests – Both or Some Parts

If an applicant fails the English section of the test or some of its parts or the Civics test, the USCIS schedules a new test date for the applicant within the next 2-3 months after the first attempt.

When the applicant reappears for the rescheduled examination, he is asked a new set of questions that are entirely different from the previous examination. Moreover, the testing officer is only required to test the applicant in the areas where he has previously failed and not require the entire test. For example, if an applicant has failed the speaking test, in the rescheduled examination, he will only be tested for the spoken English test.

If after the rescheduling, the applicant is ineligible to satisfy the officer with his answers, the officer must deny his application and state the reason for the refusal of naturalization to the applicant. Moreover, he must also state other similar reasons that might have led to the failure of the applicant, apart from his educational failure. The test results are documented in the applicant's file, which is submitted to the USCIS in either case of failure or passing of the test to have a record of the applicant testing process.

English Test – How It Works

This part of the test will require the demonstration of basic English language knowledge. The applicant must be able to demonstrate basic-level expertise in writing, reading, and speaking. It must be noted that this is not a professional English test. If an applicant fails to have a perfect command of the language and American accent, he can still be considered eligible.

This test comprises three parts that will be discussed in detail below:

Speaking Test

A designated USCIS officer will ask a few questions to the applicant and will determine his understanding of the language. The applicant's speaking ability is determined by the accuracy in terms of both grammar and content of his answers. If the applicant is unable to understand a question, the officer will repeat it and even rephrase it to ensure that the applicant completely understands it. If the applicant is unable to answer the question after repeated rephrasing, the officer will know that the applicant is unable to completely understand the English language.

If the applicant completely understands the questions asked by the officer and has enough vocabulary to answer and satisfy the officer, the applicant **passes** the speaking test.   In case the applicant is unable to give satisfactory answers, he will fail this portion. However, the applicant will still be eligible for the rest of the test, which includes writing, reading, and the civics test.

Reading Test

The candidate will be given a maximum of 3 English sentences and must be able to read at least 1 of them correctly. When the applicant correctly reads one sentence, he passes this section, and the officer proceeds to the next section. The applicant is not required to thoroughly read every word in the sentence, he or she can omit some words, and he or she can also make errors during pronunciation. As long as the meaning of the sentence remains intact, the applicant can still pass this section of the exam.

Failure of the test may be due to one of the following reasons:

- The applicant was unable to read at least 1 sentence correctly.

- He or she was making extreme pronunciation errors that resulted in changing the whole meaning of the sentence.

- He or she was taking extra time in between words to pronounce or read a single sentence.

- He or she omitted a word or used a substitute word that changed the meaning of the sentence.

Writing Test

Somewhat similar to the above section, this test requires the applicant to correctly write one of three sentences. The officer orally dictates the sentence to the applicant and the applicant is required to write it in a way that the officer can fully understand its meaning. The applicant is not allowed to use short forms for words. Once the applicant successfully writes a sentence that is understandable to the officer, the test stops.

The applicant is not required to have professional proficiency in grammar, punctuation, or spelling. He or she is only required to have a basic level of understanding and command of writing in English.

An applicant can pass the test even if he or she:

- Makes grammatical, punctuation, or spelling mistakes.

- Omit some words that do not change the meaning of the sentence.

- Write numbers in digits or English spellings.

The candidate fails the test when he or she is unable to convey the meaning of the sentence he or she has written. In short, makes enough mistakes to change the context and meaning of the sentence. Moreover, the candidate will fail the written part of the test if he or she writes:

- A completely different sentence or word.

- A short form of the given word(s).

- A sentence that does not make complete sense.

Civics Test – How It Works

As discussed earlier, an applicant who is applying for U.S. citizenship must be able to demonstrate a basic level of knowledge of civics, United States' history, and the basic principles and form of government of America.

The structure of the civics test requires the USCIS officer to ask the candidate 10 of the 100 questions that are part of the official USCIS list of civics test questions (you will find the complete list of all 100 USCIS questions with guided answers explanations in the next chapters).

To pass the exam, the candidate must correctly answer at least 6 of the 10 questions he will be asked. This test is taken to serve as an instrument of civics learning and to instill civic integrity in the applicant during his testing process.

Technically, as of today, there are 2 versions of the civics test: the 2020 version with 128 questions, and the 2008 version with 100 questions.

In practice, however, unless you have applied between December 1, 2020, and March 1, 2021, you will have to take the 2008 version of the civics exam with 100 questions.

Since USCIS has reverted back to the 2008 version due to technical/bureaucratic issues, there is an opportunity to take the 2008 version of the civics exam even for those who applied during the time period from Dec. 1, 2020, to March 1, 2021.

Following is a clarification outline.

In case of an application filed on or after December 1, 2020, and before March 1, 2021:

- If the date of the first interview is before April 19, 2021, the applicant may take the examination (or reexamination) in either the 2020 or 2008 version. It is a free choice of the applicant.

- If the date of the first Interview is on or after April 19, 2021, the applicant must take the 2008 version of the Civics test.

You must also know the following about the civics test:

- Some questions will have more than one correct answer and you will be required to provide only one of them. This means that learning only one correct answer and not going into much detail will be enough for you.

- Some questions will have a list of possible answers and you will be asked to give two correct options.

- You must be aware of the names of contemporary leaders. For example, the name of the President, Vice President, speaker of the House of Representatives, the governor of your state, etc.

- Moreover, if you are above the age of 65, you may have to study only 20 of the 100 questions, and be tested based on those. The 20 questions for people over 65 are marked with an asterisk (*). Applicants aged 50-55 and above also have the option to take the test in their language under special conditions.

These are the three subjects that the Civics test is about:

- The U.S. government
- U.S. history
- Integrated civics

As you continue reading this guide, you will find review chapters on each of these topics with all the information you need to answer each of the 100 USCIS questions.

American Government – Study Material

This chapter covers all the information you need to correctly answer each of the 57 official USCIS questions related to the topic "American Government."

Specifically, you will learn what you need to know about the principles of American democracy, the American system of government, and the rights and responsibilities of American citizens.

Principles of American Democracy

The Constitution is the supreme law of the land, which protects the basic rights of Americans. The Constitution also sets up and defines the government.

About how the Constitution defines government, the first 3 words of the Constitution "we the people" introduce the concept of self-government. In this context, "we the people" means that it is the citizens themselves who decide to create a government. The words "we the people" also indicate citizens elect representatives to make laws, and the combination of these two characteristics defines the concept of self-government.

Over time, the U.S. Constitution has undergone some changes (amendments) to improve the protection of the rights of its citizens. An amendment can be defined as a change or addition to the Constitution. The first amendment to the U.S. Constitution protects freedom of speech, assembly, press, petition to the government, and religion. The first 10 amendments made to the Constitution are called the "Bill of Rights." Despite the fact that the Constitution came into force in 1789 and has been in force for more than 200 years, to date, there have been a total of only 27 amendments to the Constitution.

Another element that played a key role in defining the principles of American democracy is the Declaration of Independence, issued on July 4, 1776.

The Declaration of Independence announced and declared the independence of the 13 British colonies on the American continent from the British Empire, officially marking the birth of the United States of America.

The Declaration of Independence established the rights to liberty, life, and the pursuit of happiness for Americans. It also established the freedom of religion, which means you can practice any religion or not practice a religion.

Since the thirteen former British colonies of the US, which are represented in the U.S. flag by 13 stripes, declared independence from Great Britain on July 4, 1776, July 4 is celebrated every year as a national holiday to commemorate the country's Independence Day.

Another element that defines the principles of American democracy is the concept of "Rule of Law." This means that everyone must follow the law, leaders must follow the law, the government must follow the law, and no one is above the law.

The setting of the economy is also important in defining the founding principles of the United States. In this regard, the United States has a capitalist economic system with a market economy.

System of Government

In accordance with the country's democratic principles, the U.S. government consists of three separate branches: legislative, executive, and judicial. Each of these branches has its own powers that are not proper to the other two. This system was constructed to prevent a single branch of government from having so much power that it could escape the control of the other two branches. This mechanism of having three separate branches, each of which has its own powers and can supervise the other two, is called "Separation of Powers" or "Checks and Balances."

The executive branch is headed by the President. The Vice President, the Cabinet (whose duties include advising the president.), and other executive departments and committees are also part of this branch. The judicial branch is in charge of reviewing laws, explaining laws, solving disputes on federal laws, and deciding whether a law goes against the Constitution or not. The Supreme Court is the most important element that makes up the judicial branch. It is the highest court in the U.S., and to date consists of nine (9) justices: one Chief Justice and eight Associate Justices. The Honorable John G. Roberts, Jr. is the current Chief Justice of the Supreme Court.

The legislative branch consists of Congress, which comprises the upper house (Senate) and lower house (House of Representatives), which together are also called the U.S. or National Legislature. They are in charge of making federal laws and other regulations.

In the U.S., every state has 2 senators, and each senator represents all the citizens of the state in which he or she is elected. Since the states that are part of the United States are 50, the senators are 100. Instead, the number of representatives varies from state to state based on the population of each state. The greater the population of a state, the more representatives will be elected to represent that state. The number of representatives in the House of Representatives is four hundred thirty-five (435).

It is to be added that the U.S. electoral system is a two-party system, which means that there are two parties that dominate the political scene and compete for supremacy. These parties are The Democratic Party and the Republican Party.

The senators are elected for a term of 6 years, and representatives are elected for 2 years.

Moreover, the U.S. Presidential elections take place every 4 years (always in November), and a President is not allowed to serve more than 2 terms. The newly elected President officially takes office on January 20 following the election, during the swearing-in ceremony known as the inauguration. This date is set by the 20th Amendment of the U.S. Constitution. Until the new President's inauguration, the outgoing President remains in office with full powers.

The Vice President is also elected for the same term, takes office during the inauguration (the same as the President) and is second in line to the U.S. President. In any emergency, if the President is unable to serve, the Vice President automatically becomes the President. In the rare event that both the President and the Vice President are unable to serve, the speaker of the House of Representatives becomes the President.

The President is the commander-in-chief of the Armed Forces. Moreover, he has the power to veto bills and sign them to become laws, while Congress may override a veto.

The Constitution, as mentioned, has divided powers among the federal government and states. The federal government has the power to print money, declare war, create an army, and make treaties, whereas the States have the power to provide schooling and other education, provide protection (police), provide safety (fire departments), give a driver's license, and approve zoning and land use.

Rights and Responsibilities

From the promulgation of the Constitution onward, four amendments were introduced that better defined who was allowed to vote and under what conditions. The combination of these amendments resulted in a picture in which every male U.S. citizen over the age of eighteen (18), regardless of race, has the right to vote. One of these 4 amendments also established that citizens did not have to pay any tax to vote.

Later, in 1920, another amendment extended the right to vote to women, as well.

As a result, today every American citizen (regardless of race or gender) over the age of 18 can vote, and this reflects the democratic nature of the country.

But while voting is certainly the main means by which Americans participate in democracy, it is not the only one. There are many others, and principal among them are helping in a campaign, participating in a community group, and publicly supporting or opposing an issue or policy.

American citizens not only have rights but also responsibilities. For example, exercising the right to vote during federal elections, although not mandatory, is so important that it is considered a citizen's responsibility. Another responsibility of American citizens is to serve on juries.

While it is true that depending on the responsibilities to which they are subject, some rights, such as the right to vote in federal elections or the right to work in federal offices, are reserved only for citizens, the United States guarantees a wide range of rights to all who live in the country. The most important of these rights are freedom of expression, speech, religion, assembly, petitioning the government, and the right to bear arms.

American citizens have the tradition of reciting the Pledge of Allegiance to show loyalty to the United States and its flag. You, too, will be required to take a similar oath at the end of your naturalization journey if you want to become an American citizen.

By the oath you take at the conclusion of your naturalization journey, however, you will also promise to renounce allegiance to other countries, to defend the Constitution and laws of the United States, to obey the law of the United States, to serve in the military, if necessary, to do important work for the nation, if necessary, and to be loyal to the United States.

Two other elements you need to know about the rights and responsibilities of American citizens in order to be successful during the exam are:

- All U.S. citizens must submit federal income tax forms by April 15 of each year.

- All citizens or immigrants between the ages of 18 and 26 must register for the Selective Service within 30 days of turning 18, or within 30 days of arriving in the U.S.

American History – Study Material

This chapter covers all the information you need to correctly answer each of the 30 official USCIS questions related to the topic "American History."

Specifically, you will learn what you need to know about American independence and the colonial period, American history of the 1800s, and current American history.

Independence and Colonial Period

The colonization of the American continent began after navigator Christopher Columbus discovered the existence of the continent and made it known to the rest of the world in 1492.

But even before colonization by Europeans began, the territory was already inhabited by the Native American populations (also known as American Indians).

Colonists reached America in search of freedom, political liberty and economic opportunity.

There were 13 colonies at the time. They were Massachusetts, Pennsylvania, Rhode Island, New Hampshire, Connecticut, New York, New Jersey, Virginia, Delaware, North Carolina, South Carolina, Georgia, and Maryland. After this land was colonized by the British, African people were taken to America and sold as slaves.

As mentioned above, the first American colonists went to America in search of freedom. But the British started oppressing the colonists by levying heavy taxes, and they were not given self-government. In addition, British soldiers began to stay in the homes of Americans, resulting in the phenomenon called "boarding" or "quartering." This convinced the colonists to fight against the British army to gain independence. The Declaration of Independence was adopted on July 4, 1776, and was written by Thomas Jefferson.

After the Declaration of Independence, as mentioned earlier, there was another key event in American history, the creation and adoption of the Constitution, drafted in 1787 by the "Founding Fathers" during the Constitutional Convention.

At the time of the drafting of the Constitution, leaders divided into two blocks: Federalists and Anti-Federalists. Those who were in favor of the Constitution and who supported it with their papers, such as James Madison, Alexander Hamilton, John Jay, and *Publius* (Publius is a pseudonym under which Hamilton, Madison, and Jay signed some of these papers) were the Federalists. They were in favor of creating a strong central government that would facilitate relations among individual states.

Those who opposed ratification of the Constitution and were advocates of a different form of government, based on small local governments, were anti-federalists.

A central figure in American history during this period was George Washington. He played a leading role in Constitution-making as well as in the American war of independence. He was also the first U.S. President and for these reasons he has been honored as the "Father of Our Country."

The 1800s

The United States, which was technically born with the Declaration of Independence (until then, it was considered 13 separate colonies), after gaining independence started to expand its territory and therefore bought the Louisiana Territory from France in 1803. The country also fought many wars during this period, such as the War of 1812, the American Civil War, the Mexican-American War, and the Spanish-American War.

Among them, the most important is the American Civil War, also known as the "War Between the States." It was an internal war between American Northern states (the United States, or Union), led by President Abraham Lincoln and Southern states (the Confederacy). The war was mainly caused by disagreeing positions on slavery, which the northern states wanted to abolish, and on other economic issues.

The war was won by the northern states, which gradually succeeded in forcing the liberation of slaves.

The most important symbol of the process of abolishing slavery was the Emancipation Proclamation, issued by President Abraham Lincoln, which established the immediate transition of millions of African Americans from slaves to freedom.

For the role he played during the Civil War, today President Lincoln is considered the savior of the Union.

Current American History

After the war era of the 1800s, the era of the 1900s was also not very peaceful. During the 1900s, the U.S. fought in both World Wars 1 & 2, the Cold War, the Korean War, the Vietnam War, and the Gulf War. This era also included the dark period of the Great Depression when America went through an economic crisis during the presidency of Franklin Roosevelt. After this era of wars, a wave of movements started across the United States for the protection and ensuring of the rights of African Americans. Under the leadership of Martin Luther King, the "Civil Rights Movement" fought for the civil rights of African Americans and demanded equal rights for all citizens. Goals that the movement was able to achieve, resulted in the extension and greater protection of several basic rights for African Americans.

One of the most important recent events in American history was the attack on the Twin Towers in New York City on September 11th, 2001, which took the lives of thousands of innocent American citizens.

Integrated Civics – Study Material

This chapter covers all the information you need to correctly answer each of the 13 official USCIS questions related to the topic "Integrated Civics."

Specifically, you will learn what you need to know about Geography, Symbols, and Holidays.

Geography

The United States is the third largest country in the world. It is bordered on the East by the Atlantic Ocean and on the West by the Pacific Ocean. The country is bordered by Canada on the North and by Mexico on the South (for a complete list of all U.S. states that border Canada and Mexico, see the answers to questions 92 and 93 of the USCIS civics questions. You will find the complete list of all 100 USCIS questions with guided answer explanations in later chapters).

The country has some of the longest rivers in the world, such as the Missouri River and the Mississippi River. The country has a varied topography and climate because of its vast land. Although each state has its capital, the capital of the country is Washington, DC. In 1886, the people of France gave a gift of friendship to the U.S. in the form of a copper statue, which is called "The statue of Liberty," installed at Liberty Island on the Hudson River in New York City.

Finally, there is a group of territories (which are called "U.S. territories" in the exam) located in the Pacific Ocean and the Caribbean Sea that, while not part of the American continent, is under the jurisdiction of the U.S. government. These territories are Puerto Rico, U.S. Virgin Islands, American Samoa, Northern Mariana Islands, and Guam.

Symbols

The American flag has 13 stripes and 50 stars. The stripes symbolize the former 13 colonies, whereas the stars symbolize the 50 American states. The American national anthem is "The Star-Spangled Banner."

Holidays

The citizens of the United States celebrate many holidays, many of which are associated with their religious beliefs, such as Christmas, Easter, etc., and some are associated with the country's history, such as Columbus Day, Independence Day (celebrated on the July 4), and Martin Luther King, Jr. Day, etc. At the same time, some holidays are associated with general celebrations, such as Thanksgiving, New Year's Eve, Labor Day, etc.

English Practice Test

As anticipated, the English test is divided into 3 parts: speaking, reading, and writing.

The Speaking Test

During the speaking test, the USCIS officer will ask you general questions on topics similar to those you have covered by filling out your application, such as zip code, family name, first name, last name, and other general information.

The officer will determine the candidate's eligibility based on the candidate's English proficiency as demonstrated by answering the questions.

In most cases, the officer can determine the speaking ability of the applicant during the formal eligibility interview on form N-400, the form to apply for naturalization. You do not need to learn historical facts or other academic material for this section. A basic understanding of the English language and the ability to answer questions understandably is enough.

The Reading Test

During the reading test, you will be asked to read up to 3 sentences. You will only need to read one of these 3 sentences correctly to pass the exam. The sentences you will be asked to read will be sentences in common use or will relate to one of the study topics. Only your knowledge of English is assessed during this exam.

The terms used in the sentences you will be asked to read in this section are based on the official USCIS Reading Vocabulary List, which you can find in full on page 34.

The Writing Test

During the writing test, you will be asked to write up to 3 sentences. You will only need to write 1 of these 3 sentences correctly to pass this section of the exam.

The sentences you will be asked to write will be sentences in common use, or will relate to one of the study topics. Only English proficiency is evaluated during this part of the exam.

The terms of the sentences you will be asked to read in this section are based on the official USCIS Writing Vocabulary List, which you can find in full on page 35.

.

To follow the official USCIS Reading Vocabulary List:

CIVICS	VERBS	OTHER (CONTENT)	HOLIDAYS	PLACES
American Flag	Can	Colors	Presidents' Day	America
Bill of Rights	Come	Dollar Bill	Memorial Day	U.S.
Capital	Do/Does	First	Flag Day	United States
Citizen	Elects	Largest	Independence Day	**PEOPLE**
City	Have/Has	Many	Labor Day	Abraham Lincoln
Congress	Is/Are/Was/Be	Most	Columbus Day	George Washington
Country	Lives/Lived	North	Thanksgiving	**QUESTION WORDS**
Father of Our Country	Meet	One	**OTHER (FUNCTION)**	How
Government	Name	People	A	What
President	Pay	Second	For	When
Right	Vote	South	Here	Where
Senators	Want		In	Who
State/States			Of	Why
White House			On	
			The	
			To	
			We	

To follow the official USCIS Writing Vocabulary List:

PEOPLE	OTHER(CONTENT)	CIVICS	VERBS	OTHER (FUNCTION)
Adams	Blue	American Indians	Can	And
Lincoln	Dollar Bill	Capital	Come	During
Washington	Fifty/50	Citizens	Elect	For
PLACES	First	Civil War	Have/Has	Here
Alaska	Largest	Congress	Is/Was/Be	In
California	Most	Father of Our Country	Lives/Lived	Of
Canada	North	Flag	Meets	On
Delaware	One	Free	Pay	The
Mexico	One Hundred /100	Freedom of Speech	Vote	To
New York City	People	President	Want	We
United States	Red	Right	**HOLIDAYS**	**MONTHS**
Washington	Second	Senators	Presidents' Day	February
Washington, D. C.	South	State/States	Memorial Day	May
	Taxes	White House	Flag Day	June
	White		Independence Day	July
			Labor Day	September
			Columbus Day	October
			Thanksgiving	November

Reading practice test 1

Below is a list of 10 sentences of the same type as those you will be asked to read on the reading exam and constructed with the same terms shown in the official USCIS Reading Vocabulary List.

Being able to read these sentences correctly implies that you are in a position to pass the reading test.

1. Who is the father of our country?

2. What is the name of our national flag?

3. Who is the current President of the United States?

4. Every American citizen has the right to vote.

5. My father lives in a southern state.

6. North and South states fought during the Civil War.

7. Senators meet during sessions of Congress.

8. We celebrate Independence Day on the 4th of July.

9. George Washington is the father of our country.

10. Abraham Lincoln was the 16th U.S. President.

Reading practice test 2

Below is a list of 10 sentences of the same type as those you will be asked to read on the reading exam and constructed with the same terms as shown in the official USCIS Reading Vocabulary List. Being able to read these sentences correctly implies that you are in a position to pass the reading test.

1. I want to vote.

2. Why are there only 100 senators?

3. Why is Columbus Day celebrated?

4. Give me a one-dollar bill.

5. People celebrate Thanksgiving every year.

6. Where is the largest state of the United States?

7. Who will pay for me?

8. It is my right to vote.

9. There are three colors in our flag.

10. I want to meet the President.

Writing practice test 1

Below, is a list of 10 sentences of the same type as those you will be asked to write during the writing exam and constructed with the same terms shown in the official USCIS Writing Vocabulary List. Practice by asking someone next to you to read each sentence to you and try writing it. When you have finished writing, go back and look at sentences from the examples to check that you have written them correctly.

1. The President of the United States celebrated Thanksgiving.

2. I visited my family in New York City.

3. South and North states fought during the Civil War on slavery.

4. A hundred people protested outside the White House.

5. Freedom of speech is a basic human right.

6. George Washington is the father of our country.

7. The right to vote was granted to citizens of the United States.

8. Citizens of the United States have freedom of speech.

9. Can you give me a 100-dollar bill?

10. Washington, D.C., is the capital of the United States.

Writing practice test 2

Below, is a list of 10 sentences of the same type as those you will be asked to write during the writing exam and constructed with the same terms shown in the official USCIS Writing Vocabulary List. Practice by asking someone next to you to read each sentence to you and try writing it. When you have finished writing, go back and look at sentences from the examples to check that you have written them correctly.

1. Americans celebrate Columbus Day every year.

2. My grandmother meets us on Thanksgiving.

3. Every American citizen must pay his taxes.

4. I will visit Mexico during the holidays.

5. A red flag is a sign of danger.

6. My sister lives in California.

7. Labor Day is celebrated on the first Monday in September.

8. Abraham Lincoln was the 16th President of the United States.

9. American citizens are free to follow any religion.

10. There are 100 senators in the upper house of Congress.

Speaking practice test 1 - questions

This section comprises a set of questions replicating those you will be asked during the first part of the Interview, the one where the USCIS officer will ask you questions that, in most cases, relate to topics similar to those addressed by filling out the naturalization application.

By identifying the correct answers in this section, it will become easier for you to answer the questions during the real Interview.

1. **Mr. John Fitzgerald Kennedy was the 35th President of the United States.**

   a) *What is Mr. John Fitzgerald Kennedy's first name?*

   _____

   b) *What is Mr. John Fitzgerald Kennedy's family/last name?*

   _____

   c) *What is Mr. John Fitzgerald Kennedy's middle name?*

   _____

2. **Alex was born in Canada but now lives in Texarkana, Texas. Her address is 688 Hall Place, Apt. C6, Texarkana, Texas 75503**

   a) *What is Alex's country of birth?*

   _____

   b) *Where does Alex currently live?*

   _____

c) *What is Alex's street name?*

_____

d) *What is Alex's apartment number?*

_____

e) *What is Alex's zip code?*

_____

3. **Bill is a carpenter at Custom Hardwood Doors. He has been working there for 3 years.**

a) *What is the name of Bill's Employer?*

_____

b) *What is Bill's occupation?*

_____

4. **Bob has two daughters and a son. His wife divorced him last month.**

a) *How many children does Bob have?*

_____

b) *What is Bob's marital status?*

_____

5. **Marisa is living in Chicago, Illinois,. Previously, she lived in Philadelphia, Pennsylvania.**

a) *Where does Marisa live now?*

_____

b) Where did Marisa live before that?

_____

6. **Every year, Jeff takes three trips. He goes to Bali, Indonesia, for recreation every summer for a month. He visits his parents in Florida during Christmas for 10 days. He also visits his friends in Italy for a week.**

a) How much time does Jeff spend outside the U.S. every year?

_____

b) How many trips does he take outside the U.S.?

_____

c) Which two countries does Jeff visit each year?

_____

d) Where does he go in summer?

_____

e) How many trips does he take inside the US?

_____

f) Which U.S. states does Jeff visit each year?

_____

Speaking practice test 1 - answers

- **Question 1**

    a) John

    b) Kennedy

    c) Fitzgerald

- **Question 2**

    a) Canada

    b) Texas

    c) Hall place

    d) C6

    e) 75503

- **Question 3**

    a) Custom Hardwood Doors

    b) Carpenter

- **Question 4**

    a) 3

    b) Divorced

- **Question 5**

    a) Chicago

    b) Pennsylvania

- **Question 6**

    a) 5 weeks

    b) 2 trips

    c) Italy and Indonesia

    d) Bali, Indonesia

    e) One

    f) Florida

Speaking practice test 2 – questions

Similar to speaking test 1, this is another simulation that replicates sentences similar to those you might hear or have to say during the exam. The goal of this test is to select the sentence that has a similar meaning to the main sentence.

Recognizing the right answer in this test makes you develop skills that will greatly help you answer the USCIS officer correctly.

1. **Anna <u>rarely</u> misses school.**

    a) Anna occasionally misses school.

    b) Anna never misses school.

    c) Anna always misses school.

2. **Let me <u>verify</u> this question.**

    a) Let me see if the information is true.

    b) Let me know if the information is true.

    c) Let me check if the information is true.

3. **Bob, can you tell me your <u>marital status</u>?**

    a) Tell me if you are living on rent.

    b) Tell me if you are married, separated, divorced, widowed, or single.

    c) Tell me if you are an American citizen.

4. **I <u>swear</u> to honor the flag.**

    a) I promise to honor the flag.

    b) I say to honor the flag.

    c) I think to honor the flag.

5. Maria <u>registered</u> for the drama club.

   a) Maria signed up for the drama club.

   b) Maria went to the drama club.

   c) Maria requested the drama club.

6. How is your <u>spouse</u> doing?

   a) How is your daughter or son doing?

   b) How is your brother or sister doing?

   c) How is your husband or wife doing?

7. Can you tell me your <u>current address?</u>

   a) Where are you from?

   b) Where do you live?

   c) Where is your hometown?

8. Kindly tell me your <u>date of birth</u>.

   a) The date when you were born.

   b) The date of your marriage.

   c) The date of your registration.

9. Jason <u>advocates</u> the Black Lives Matter movement.

   a) Jason demands the Black Lives Matter movement.

   b) Jason supports the Black Lives Matter movement.

   c) Jason follows the Black Lives Matter movement.

10. James <u>failed to </u>appear in court.

   a) James appears early in court.

   b) James did not appear in court.

   c) James stopped appearing in court.

11. I live near a <u>federal</u> government building.

    a) I live near a private building.

    b) I live near a public building.

    c) I live near the U.S. government building.

12. You are <u>exempt</u> from the test.

    a) You do not have to take the test.

    b) You must take the exam.

    c) You failed the exam.

13. Do you have any <u>prior</u> experience in dancing?

    a) Do you dance?

    b) Do you go to dance?

    c) Have you danced before?

14. The status of the application is still <u>pending</u>.

    a) The application has not been approved yet.

    b) The application has been approved.

    c) The application has been rejected.

15. <u>Have you ever</u> taken an interview?

    a) Do you know what an interview is?

    b) In your lifetime, have you taken any interviews?

    c) Can you take an interview?

16. Jason is a <u>member</u> of the football club.

    a) Jason belongs to the football club.

    b) Jason follows the football club.

    c) Jason likes the football club.

17. Jason is a <u>resident</u> of the United States.

    a) Jason currently lives in the United States.

    b) Jason used to live in the United States.

    c) Jason will be living in the United States.

18. I <u>requested</u> the officer to provide me with the necessary information.

    a) I demanded the officer for the necessary information.

    b) I ordered the officer for necessary information.

    c) I asked the officer for the necessary information.

19. Anaya's <u>disability</u> does not prevent her from enjoying life.

    a) Anaya cannot enjoy life.

    b) Anaya has a physical disability, but it does not prevent her from enjoying life.

    c) Anaya does not enjoy life.

20. How many <u>dependents</u> do you have?

    a) How many people are you financially supporting?

    b) How many people are supporting you?

    c) How many people are living with you?

Speaking practice test 2 – answers

1. a) Anna occasionally misses school.

2. c) Let me check if the information is true.

3. b) Tell me if you are married, separated, divorced, widowed, or single.

4. a) I promise to honor the flag.

5. a) Maria signed up for the drama club.

6. c) How is your husband or wife doing?

7. b) Where do you live?

8. a) The date when you were born.

9. b) Jason supports the Black Lives Matter movement.

10. b) James did not appear in court.

11. c) I live near the U.S. government building.

12. a) You do not have to take the test.

13. c) Have you danced before?

14. a) The application has not been approved yet.

15. b) In your lifetime, have you taken any interviews?

16. a) Jason belongs to the football club.

17. a) Jason currently lives in the United States.

18. c) I asked the officer for the necessary information.

19. b) Anaya has a physical disability, but it does not prevent her from enjoying life.

20. a) How many people are you financially supporting?

Bonus Flashcards

Dear future American citizen, we are grateful for the trust you are giving us by preparing for the Naturalization Test with our Study Guide. That is why we are happy to share this exclusive and extremely valuable content with you!

Here the 2 main advantages of using our Flashcards:

- Help to store information quickly, facilitating long-term memorization through the "active recall" process, which involves recalling in your mind the same information over and over again. Which is exactly what happens when you train with Flashcards.

- Give you a clear idea of the questions you will be asked in the actual test. This way, your mind will already be used to the test you will face, giving you the right peace of mind to do it without the slightest anxiety. Which often makes the difference between passing or failing.

Are you ready to add this powerful tool to your exam-taking toolbox?

Scan the QR code and get your 100 bonus Flashcards right away:

Dear Future American Citizen,

first of all, thank you again for purchasing our product.

Secondly, congratulations! If you are using our Guide, you are among those few who are willing to do whatever it takes to excel on the exam and are not satisfied with just trying.

We create our Study Guides in the same spirit. We want to offer our students only the best to help them get only the best through precise, accurate, and easy-to-use information.

That is why **your success is our success**, and if you think our Guide helped you achieve your goals, we would love it if you could take 60 seconds of your time to leave us a review on Amazon.

Thank you again for trusting us by choosing our Guide, and good luck with your new life as a U.S. citizen.

Sincerely,
H.S. Test Preparation Team

Scan the QR code to leave a review (it only takes you 60 seconds):

The 100 USCIS Questions with Guided Answer Explanation

In this chapter, you will be provided with the set of 100 official USCIS civics questions taken from the 2008 Civics test, which is what is still in use today in 2024-2025 unless you have applied between December 1, 2020, and March 1, 2021 (refer to chapter "Civics Test – How It Works" for more details). You will also be provided with an explanation for each question. Note that these questions will be asked verbally by the designated USCIS officer. You will NOT be asked all 100 questions. Instead, you will be asked a random set of 10 questions, and you will be expected to correctly answer 6 of these questions.

Civics Questions for the Naturalization Test

(Note: The questions in this section are taken from the official USCIS list. If you are familiar with U.S. history or have general information on the subject, you might know alternative answers to some of the questions. However, USCIS encourages that you answer with the options given in this section). Keep in mind that it is not necessary to give all the answers listed in the section below. It is sufficient to give only one answer unless otherwise specified in the question or explicitly asked by the examiner.

If you are above the age of 65, you may have to study only 20 of the 100 questions, and be tested based on those. The 20 questions for people over 65 are marked with an asterisk (*).

American Government

Principles of American Democracy

1. *What is the supreme law of the land?*

- The Constitution

Explanation: The United States of America's Constitution is the country's supreme law. It is the foundation of all federal authorities and imposes significant limitations on the executive branch that safeguard Americans' fundamental freedoms. It was outlined with the cooperation of the state legislative and the sovereign authority of the people.

2. *What does the Constitution do?*

- Sets up the government

- Defines the government

- Protects basic rights of Americans

Explanation: The Constitution outlines the three main federal government branches and their respective responsibilities. It also specifies the fundamental legislation of the United States federal government.

3. *The idea of self-government is in the first three words of the Constitution. What are these words?*

- We the People

Explanation: The first 3 words of the Constitution "we the people" introduce the concept of self-government. In this context, "we the people" means that it is the citizens themselves who decide to create a government. The words "we the people" also indicate citizens elect representatives to make laws, and the combination of these two characteristics defines the concept of self-government.

4. What is an amendment?

- A change (to the Constitution)

- An addition (to the Constitution)

Explanation: An amendment can be defined as a change or addition to the Constitution.

5. What do we call the first ten amendments to the Constitution?

- The Bill of Rights

Explanation: The first ten (10) Amendments to the Constitution are known as the Bill of Rights. They describe the rights Americans have with regard to their government. They safeguard the individual's civil rights and liberties, such as freedom of speech, press, assembly, and religion.

6. What is <u>one</u> right or freedom from the First Amendment? *

- Speech

- Religion

- Assembly

- Press

- Petition the government

Explanation: The first amendment to the U.S. Constitution protects freedom of speech, assembly, press, religion, and petition to the government.

7. How many amendments does the Constitution have?

- Twenty-seven (27)

Explanation: With time, the American Constitution has adopted changes (amendments) to improve the protection of the rights of its citizens. To date, there have been 27 amendments to the Constitution.

8. What did the Declaration of Independence do?

- Announced our independence (from Great Britain)

- Declared our independence (from Great Britain)

- Said that the United States is free (from Great Britain)

Explanation: The thirteen former colonies of the U.S. declared independence from the British Empire through the Declaration of Independence on July 4, 1776. The Declaration of Independence announced the U.S.'s independence from the British Empire and declared the country free.

9. What are two rights in the Declaration of Independence?

- Life

- Liberty

- Pursuit of happiness

Explanation: *"We hold these Truths to be self-evident, that all Men are created equal, that they are endowed by their Creator with certain unalienable, that among these are Life, Liberty and the pursuit of happiness."* – from the Declaration of Independence

10. What is freedom of religion?

- You can practice any religion, or not practice a religion

Explanation: Religious freedom is the right to follow or not follow any religion. It is a provision of the First Amendment to the United States Constitution and applies to anyone who lives in the United States.

11. What is the economic system in the United States? *

- Capitalist economy

- Market economy

Explanation: The economic system of the United States is a mix of capitalist economy and market economy. In the U.S. economy, both privately owned enterprises and the government play important roles.

12. What is the "Rule of Law"?

- Everyone must follow the law

- Leaders must obey the law

- Government must obey the law

- No one is above the law

Explanation: The "Rule of Law" is the concept that expresses how everyone must be subject to the same laws (including governments, legislators, and leaders), that everyone is equal in front of the law, and no one is above the law.

System of Government

13. Name <u>one</u> branch or part of the government. *

- Congress

- Legislative

- President

- Executive

- The courts

- Judicial

Explanation: the U.S. government consists of three separate branches: legislative, executive, and judicial. Judges depend on the government's executive branch to enforce court decisions.

14. What stops <u>one</u> branch of government from becoming too powerful?

- Checks and balances

- Separation of powers

Explanation: The U.S. government consists of three separate branches: legislative, executive, and judicial. Each of these branches has its own powers that are not proper to the other two. This system was constructed to prevent a single branch of government from having so much power that it could escape the control of the other two branches. This mechanism of having three separate branches, each of which has its own powers and can supervise the other two, is called "Separation of Powers" or "Checks and Balances."

15. Who is in charge of the executive branch?

- The President

Explanation: The executive branch is headed by the President. Vice President and other executive departments and committees are also part of this branch.

16. Who makes federal laws?

- Congress

- Senate and House (of Representatives)

- (U.S. or national) legislature

Explanation: Congress, which comprises the Senate and House of Representatives, has the power to make federal laws. Together, the Senate and the House can also be defined as the legislature.

17. What are the two parts of the U.S. Congress? *

- The Senate (or upper house) and the House (or House of Representatives)

Explanation: Together, the upper house (Senate) and lower house (House of Representatives) form Congress, which forms, in turn, the legislative branch of the United States.

18. How many U.S. Senators are there?

- One hundred (100)

Explanation: Each state has 2 senators, while the number of representatives varies from state to state based on the population of each state.
Since there are 50 states in the United States and each state elects 2 senators, the Senate consists of a total of one hundred (100) senators.
Senators are elected for a term of 6 years, whereas the representatives are elected for 2 years. Senators are allowed to run for as many terms as they choose. Their responsibility in the Senate is to represent all of the citizens in their state (Similar explanation for questions: 19, 22, 23, and 24).

19. We elect a U.S. Senator for how many years?

- Six (6)

20. Who is <u>one</u> of your state's U.S. Senators now? *

- Answers will vary. District of Columbia residents and residents of U.S. territories should answer that D.C. (or the territory where the applicant lives) has no U.S. Senators.

- Scan this QR code for a complete list of all U.S. senators:

21. The House of Representatives has how many voting members?

- Four hundred thirty-five (435)

22. We elect a U.S. Representative for how many years?

- Two (2)

23. Name your U.S. Representative.

- Answers will vary. Residents of territories with nonvoting Delegates or Resident Commissioners may provide the name of that Delegate or Commissioner. Also acceptable is any statement that the territory has no (voting) Representatives in Congress.

- Scan this QR code for a complete list of all U.S. Representatives:

24. Who does a U.S. Senator represent?

- All the people in the state where he was elected

25. Why do some states have more Representatives than other states?

- (because of) the state's population

- (because) they have more people

- (because) some states have more people

Explanation: Each state elects a number of representatives that increases as the population increases. The greater the state's population, the more candidates that state can elect. The United States government conducts a census every 10 years to count the citizens of the United States. The census determines the total number of people in each state. It also determines how many representatives can be elected within each individual state. Districts are used to partition the state. One representative is elected in each district.

26. We elect a President for how many years?

- Four (4)

Explanation: The twenty-second Amendment, ratified in 1951, restricts Presidents to two four-year terms. No one can serve more than two four-year terms as President.

27. In what month do we vote for President? *

- November

Explanation: Presidential elections are always in November. In 1845, Congress declared November was the ideal month for elections. At the time, the majority of Americans lived on farms. Farmers had finished harvesting their crops by November, which made it easier for them to go out and vote. November was also not as severe as the winter season.

28. What is the name of the President of the United States now? *

- Joseph R. Biden, Jr.

- Joe Biden

- Biden

Explanation: The current President of the U.S. as of 2021 is Joe Biden. However, the President changes on January 20 following the election. Therefore, you must know the name of the current President at the time you are taking the exam. The updates on the most recent President can be acquired by scanning the following QR code:

29. What is the name of the Vice President of the United States now?

- Kamala D. Harris

- Kamala Harris

- Harris

Explanation: The current Vice President of the U.S. as of 2021 is Kamala Harris. However, the Vice President changes on January 20 following the election. Therefore, you must know the name of the current Vice President at the time you are taking the exam. The updates on the most recent Vice President can be acquired by scanning the following QR code:

30. If the President can no longer serve, who becomes President?

- The Vice President

Explanation: If the President is unable to serve, the Vice President becomes the President. In the event that both the President and Vice President are unable to serve, the speaker of the House of Representatives becomes the president.

31. If both the President and the Vice President can no longer serve, who becomes President?

- The Speaker of the House

Explanation: Same explanation for question 30

32. Who is the Commander in Chief of the military?

- The President

33. Who signs bills to become laws?

- The President

34. Who vetoes bills?

- The President

35. What does the President's Cabinet do?

- Advises the President

Explanation: The cabinet advises the President on important issues and bills. It consists of the Vice President and the heads of 15 executive departments (which in other legal systems may be called ministries).

36. What are _two_ Cabinet-level positions?

- Secretary of Agriculture

- Secretary of Commerce

- Secretary of Defense

- Secretary of Education

- Secretary of Energy

- Secretary of Health and Human Services

- Secretary of Homeland Security

- Secretary of Housing and Urban Development

- Secretary of the Interior

- Secretary of Labor

- Secretary of State

- Secretary of Transportation

- Secretary of the Treasury

- Secretary of Veterans Affairs

- Attorney General

- Vice President

37. What does the judicial branch do?

- Reviews laws

- Explains laws

- Resolves disputes (disagreements)

- Decides if a law goes against the Constitution

38. What is the highest court in the United States?

- The Supreme Court

Explanation: The Supreme Court is the country's highest court. The Supreme Court considers if a law violates the Constitution. All other courts must follow the rules laid down by the Supreme Court. The Supreme Court's judgment has to be followed by all states.

39. How many justices are on the Supreme Court?

- Nine (9)

Explanation: The present Supreme Court has nine justices: one Chief Justice and eight Associate Justices.
For up-to-date information on the number of justices, scan the following QR code:

40. Who is the Chief Justice of the United States now?

- John Roberts

- John G. Roberts, Jr.

Explanation: The current Chief Justice of the U.S. as of 2005 is John G. Roberts. However, the Chief Justice changes. You must know the name of the current Chief Justice at the time you are taking the exam. The updates on the most recent Chief Justice can be acquired by scanning the following QR code:

41. Under our Constitution, some powers belong to the federal government. What is <u>one</u> power of the federal government?

- To print money

- To declare war

- To create an army

- To make treaties

42. Under our Constitution, some powers belong to the states. What is <u>one</u> power of the states?

- Provide schooling and education

- Provide protection (police)

- Provide safety (fire departments)

- Give a driver's license

- Approve zoning and land use

43. Who is the Governor of your state now?

- Answers will vary. District of Columbia residents should answer that D.C. does not have a Governor.

- Scan the QR code for a complete list of all governors:

44. What is the capital of your state? *

- Answers will vary. District of Columbia residents should answer that D.C. is not a state and does not have a capital. Residents of U.S. territories should name the capital of the territory.

- Below, a complete list of all the capitals of the United States

State	Capital	State	Capital
Alabama	Montgomery	Iowa	Des Moines
Alaska	Juneau	Kansas	Topeka
Arizona	Phoenix	Kentucky	Frankfort
Arkansas	Little Rock	Louisiana	Baton Rouge
California	Sacramento	Maine	Augusta
Colorado	Denver	Maryland	Annapolis
Connecticut	Hartford	Massachusetts	Boston
Delaware	Dover	Michigan	Lansing
Florida	Tallahassee	Minnesota	Saint Paul
Georgia	Atlanta	Mississippi	Jackson
Hawaii	Honolulu	Missouri	Jefferson City
Idaho	Boise	Montana	Helena
Illinois	Springfield	Nebraska	Lincoln
Indiana	Indianapolis	Nevada	Carson City

State	Capital
New Hampshire	Concord
New Jersey	Trenton
New Mexico	Santa Fe
New York	Albany
North Carolina	Raleigh
North Dakota	Bismarck
Ohio	Columbus
Oklahoma	Oklahoma City
Oregon	Salem
Pennsylvania	Harrisburg
Rhode Island	Providence

State	Capital
South Carolina	Columbia
South Dakota	Pierre
Tennessee	Nashville
Texas	Austin
Utah	Salt Lake City
Vermont	Montpelier
Virginia	Richmond
Washington	Olympia
West Virginia	Charleston
Wisconsin	Madison
Wyoming	Cheyenne

45. What are the __two__ major political parties in the United States? *

- Democratic and Republican

Explanation: The two largest political parties in the United States are the Democratic Party and the Republican Party. The Democrats are represented by a donkey symbol. The Republican Party is represented by an elephant symbol.

46. What is the political party of the President now?

- Democratic (party)

Explanation: For information on the latest President's party at the time of the test, scan the following QR code:

47. What is the name of the Speaker of the House of Representatives now?

- Mike Johnson

- Johnson

- James Michael Johnson (birth name)

Explanation: James Michael Johnson is an American politician and member of the Republican Party. He was elected 57th speaker of the House of Representatives on October 25, 2023. Born on January 30, 1972, he represents Louisiana's 4th congressional district in the House of Representatives and is now in his fourth term. For information on the latest *Speaker of the House of Representatives* at the time of the test, scan the following QR code:

Rights and Responsibilities

48. There are four amendments to the Constitution about who can vote. Describe <u>one</u> of them.

- Citizens eighteen (18) and older (can vote)

- You don't have to pay (a poll tax) to vote

- Any citizen can vote. (Women and men can vote.)

- A male citizen of any race (can vote)

Explanation: Since independence, 4 amendments have been made to the Constitution of the U.S. to ensure the right to vote.

49. What is <u>one</u> responsibility that is only for United States citizens? *

- Serve on a jury

- Vote in a federal election

Explanation: Citizens of the United States are qualified to vote in federal elections. Voting is essential. However, there is no law forcing citizens to vote. It is solely a moral responsibility. Instead, there is an obligation for citizens to serve on juries when called upon. If a citizen receives a summons to serve on a jury, he or she must comply. A jury is a group of persons who sit in a courtroom to hear a trial. The outcome of the trial is decided by the voting of the jury.

50. Name <u>one</u> right only for United States citizens.

- Vote in a federal election

- Run for federal office

Explanation: Only citizens of the United States are eligible to vote and apply for state offices. Through their chosen representatives, citizens make laws. There are several legislators and senators in the United States who were naturalized citizens. Naturalized citizens, however, are unable to become President.

51. What are <u>two</u> rights of everyone living in the United States?

- Freedom of expression

- Freedom of speech

- Freedom of assembly

- Freedom to petition the government

- Freedom of religion

- The right to bear arms

52. What do we show loyalty to when we say the Pledge of Allegiance?

- The United States

- The flag

Explanation: As an American citizen, you are expected to pledge allegiance to show loyalty to the flag and the United States of America. You also pledge to stay loyal to the country, defend and obey the Constitution and the law of the land, and serve the nation when and if needed.

53. What is <u>one</u> promise you make when you become a United States citizen?

- Give up loyalty to other countries

- Defend the Constitution and laws of the United States

- Obey the laws of the United States

- Serve in the U.S. military (if needed)

- Serve (do important work for) the nation (if needed)

- Be loyal to the United States

Explanation: To become a U.S. citizen, after passing the exam, you will have to take an oath. During this oath, you will make a series of promises (listed above) that should make explicit your loyalty to the United States.

54. How old do citizens have to be to vote for President? *

- Eighteen (18) and older

Explanation: To vote for President, citizens must be 18 years old or older. The Twenty-sixth Amendment was added to the Constitution by Congress and the states in 1971 because the younger generation had broadened its civic and political awareness and so it was considered appropriate to allow them to vote.

55. What are <u>two</u> ways that Americans can participate in their democracy?

- Vote

- Join a political party

- Help with a campaign

- Join a civic group

- Join a community group

- Give an elected official your opinion on

  an issue

- Call Senators and Representatives

- Publicly support or oppose an issue or

  policy

- Run for office

- Write to a newspaper

56. When is the last day you can send in federal income tax forms? *

- April 15

Explanation: If you file a calendar year tax return and your tax year ends on December 31, the deadline to file your federal individual income tax return usually is April 15 every year.

57. When must all men register for the Selective Service?

- At age eighteen (18)

- Between eighteen (18) and twenty-six (26)

Explanation: Between the ages of 18 and 26, all men must register for the Selective Service. As you enroll, you are telling the government that you are willing to engage in military service if needed. You are not required to engage in military service unless you wish to do so.

American History

Colonial Period and Independence

58. What is *one* reason colonists came to America?

- Freedom

- Political liberty

- Religious freedom

- Economic opportunity

- Practice their religion

- Escape persecution

Explanation: The colonists had come to America in search of freedom. Sometimes, they wanted to escape different forms of persecution and have political liberty and be able to practice their religion freely.

59. Who lived in America before the Europeans arrived?

- American Indians

- Native Americans

Explanation: Native Americans (also American Indians) lived in America before the Europeans arrived on this land and colonized it.

60. What group of people was taken to America and sold as slaves?

- Africans

- People from Africa

Explanation: In the early 1500s, millions of people from Africa were brought to America as slaves. Slave masters considered slaves as property for hundreds of years. This was a significant contributing factor to the Civil War. After the Civil War ended in 1865, slavery was abolished. People who had been slaves gained freedom.

61. Why did the colonists fight the British?

- Because of high taxes (taxation without representation)

- Because the British army stayed in their houses (boarding, quartering)

- Because they didn't have self-government

Explanation: The colonists migrated to America in search of freedom. But the British started oppressing them by levying heavy taxes and not allowing them self-government. In addition, British soldiers began to occupy the homes of Americans. This convinced the Americans to fight against the British.

62. Who wrote the Declaration of Independence?

- (Thomas) Jefferson

63. When was the Declaration of Independence adopted?

- July 4, 1776

Explanation to questions 62 & 63: The Declaration of Independence was approved by the colonies on July 4, 1776. The Declaration of Independence was written by Thomas Jefferson. It claimed that the colonies were liberated from British rule. The Declaration was signed by representatives from the 13 colonies. July 4, 1776, therefore, is considered as the date when the United States of America was officially born as an independent nation.

64. There were 13 original states. Name <u>three</u>.

- New Hampshire

- Massachusetts

- Rhode Island

- Connecticut

- New York

- New Jersey

- Pennsylvania

- Delaware

- Maryland

- Virginia

- North Carolina

- South Carolina

- Georgia

Explanation: New Hampshire, Massachusetts, Rhode Island, Connecticut, New York, New Jersey, Pennsylvania, Delaware, Maryland, Virginia, North Carolina, South Carolina, and Georgia were the first 13 states. The thirteen initial states were the earliest thirteen British territories. To answer this question correctly, you only need to remember the name of 3 out of 13 colonies.

65. What happened at the Constitutional Convention?

- The Constitution was written

- The Founding Fathers wrote the Constitution

Explanation: After the Declaration of Independence, the Constitution was drafted by the "Founding Fathers" during the "Constitutional Convention" in 1787. Fifty-five delegates from 12 of the original 13 states attended the Convention to discuss the system of government and draft the U.S. Constitution. The states decided to approve the Constitution after the Constitutional Convention.

66. When was the Constitution written?

- 1787

67. The Federalist Papers supported the passage of the U.S. Constitution. Name <u>one</u> of the writers.

- (James) Madison

- (Alexander) Hamilton

- (John) Jay

- Publius

Explanation: At the time of the drafting of the Constitution, leaders were divided into two blocs: Federalists and Anti-Federalists. Those who were in favor of the Constitution and who supported it with their "papers," such as James Madison, Alexander Hamilton, and John Jay (the three often wrote under the collective pseudonym "Publius") were the Federalists.

68. What is <u>one</u> thing Benjamin Franklin is famous for?

- U.S. diplomat

- Oldest member of the Constitutional Convention

- First Postmaster General of the United States

- Writer of "Poor Richard's Almanac"

- Started the first free libraries

69. Who is the "Father of Our Country"?

- (George) Washington

Explanation: The role George Washington played during the Revolutionary War meant that he was recognized from that time onward as the "Father of Our Country".

70. Who was the first President? *

- (George) Washington

Explanation: George Washington played a leading role in Constitution-making as well as in the American war of independence. He was also the first United States President and, for these reasons, he has been honored as the "Father of Our Country".

1800s

71. What territory did the United States buy from France in 1803?

- The Louisiana Territory

- Louisiana

Explanation: After gaining independence, the United States started to expand its territory and therefore bought The Louisiana Territory, or Louisiana, from France in 1803.

72. Name one war fought by the United States in the 1800s.

- War of 1812

- Mexican-American War

- Civil War

- Spanish-American War

Explanation: For more information on this topic, refer to the chapter "American History - Study Material.".

73. Name the U.S. war between the North and the South.

- The Civil War

- The War between the States

Explanation: It was an internal war between American Northern states (the United States, or Union), led by President Abraham Lincoln, and Southern states (the Confederacy). The war was mainly caused by disagreeing positions on slavery, which the northern states wanted to abolish, and on other economic issues.
The war was won by the northern states, which gradually succeeded in forcing the liberation of slaves.

74. Name one problem that led to the Civil War.

- Slavery

- Economic reasons

- States' rights

Explanation: The Civil War started as a result of disputes concerning slavery and other matters, such as economic concerns and states' rights. Some people thought that slavery should be prohibited, while others did not. Enslaved African Americans were used as labor on farms and in cities when the Civil War began in 1861. Many individuals in the South thought that slaves were necessary for their economy and everyday lives. At the same time, people in the North wanted slavery to be abolished. The South fought the Civil War in order to preserve the legality of slavery. In 1865, the North won the war. Slavery was made illegal in every state. (same explanation applies to questions: 75 & 76)

75. What was <u>one</u> important thing that Abraham Lincoln did? *

- Freed the slaves (Emancipation Proclamation)

- Saved (or preserved) the Union

- Led the United States during the Civil War

76. What did the Emancipation Proclamation do?

- Freed the slaves

- Freed slaves in the Confederacy

- Freed slaves in the Confederate states

- Freed slaves in most Southern states

77. What did Susan B. Anthony do?

- Fought for women's rights

- Fought for civil rights

Explanation: Susan B. Anthony was a key figure in the women's rights movement and civil rights movement. She delivered talks in favor of women's rights, notably the right to vote. In 1872 Susan B. Anthony even attempted to vote and was arrested. After her death in 1906, the struggle continued, and the Nineteenth Amendment, which granted women the right to vote, was added to the Constitution in 1920.

Recent American History and Other Important Historical Information

78. Name <u>one</u> war fought by the United States in the 1900s. *

- World War I

- World War II

- Korean War

- Vietnam War

- (Persian) Gulf War

Explanation: During the 1900s, the U.S. fought in both World Wars 1 & 2, the Cold War, the Korean War, the Vietnam War, and the Gulf War.

79. Who was President during World War I?

- (Woodrow) Wilson

Explanation: Woodrow Wilson was the American President at the time of World War I. He did not join the war until late 1917.

80. Who was President during the Great Depression and World War II?

- (Franklin) Roosevelt

Explanation: Elected in 1933, Franklin D. Roosevelt was the President of the United States during the Great Depression and World War II. The term "Great Depression" is used to refer to the period, from 1929 to 1939, during which the U.S. economy fell precipitously, banks went bankrupt, and many people were unemployed. Franklin D. Roosevelt attempted to repair the economy. In 1941, the United States entered World War II. Americans fought alongside Great Britain, the Soviet Union, France, and China against Germany, Italy, and Japan. Franklin D. Roosevelt served as President until his death in 1945.

81. Who did the United States fight in World War II?

- Japan, Germany, and Italy

Explanation: In World War Two, the U.S. fought against Germany, Italy, and Japan. After Japan bombed Pearl Harbor (Hawaii) in 1941, the United States entered World War II. Germany and Italy had Japan as an ally. They joined forces to create the "Axis powers." In 1945, the U.S. and its allies defeated Japan, Germany, and Italy.

82. Before he was President, Eisenhower was a general. What war was he in?

- World War II

Explanation: During World War II, President Dwight D. Eisenhower served as a general, and commanded the American Army and the allied forces in Western Europe. He was a popular military hero when he returned from WWII. In 1953, he was elected President.

83. During the Cold War, what was the main concern of the United States?

- Communism

Explanation: After the end of World War II, The U.S. and USSR started a cold war that was an ideological war between communism and capitalism. The United States was concerned about the spread of communism to other countries. The United States wanted to spread freedom and liberty in the world through democracy and capitalism.

84. What movement tried to end racial discrimination?

- Civil rights (movement)

Explanation: From 1954 through 1968, the civil rights movement was a political ideology and movement in the United States to end structural racial segregation, discrimination, and marginalization throughout the country. One of the most important leaders of this movement was Martin Luther King, Jr.

85. What did Martin Luther King, Jr. do? *

- Fought for civil rights

- Worked for equality for all Americans

Explanation: Under the leadership of Martin Luther King, Jr., Americans fought for the freedom and civil rights of African Americans and demanded equal rights for all citizens which were ensured, and African Americans were given voting and other fundamental rights.

86. What major event happened on September 11, 2001, in the United States?

- Terrorists attacked the United States

Explanation: It was one of the most tragic events in American history. The terrorist attack on the Twin Towers in New York City on September 11th, 2001, took the lives of thousands of innocent American citizens.

87. Name <u>one</u> American Indian tribe in the United States.

- Cherokee
- Navajo
- Sioux
- Chippewa
- Choctaw
- Pueblo
- Apache
- Iroquois
- Creek
- Blackfeet
- Seminole

- Cheyenne
- Arawak
- Shawnee
- Mohegan
- Huron
- Oneida
- Lakota
- Crow
- Teton
- Hopi
- Inuit

Integrated Civics

Geography

88. Name <u>one</u> of the two longest rivers in the United States.

- Missouri (River)

- Mississippi (River)

Explanation: The Missouri River and the Mississippi River are the two longest rivers in the United States. The Missouri River is the longest river in the United States. It originates in the Rocky Mountains and runs 2,341 miles, first eastward and then southward before flowing into the Mississippi River. The Mississippi River flows through 10 states in the United States. It begins in Minnesota, near the border with Canada. It concludes in Louisiana.

89. What ocean is on the West Coast of the United States?

- Pacific (Ocean)

Explanation: The Pacific Ocean bathes the entire west coast of the United States.

90. What ocean is on the East Coast of the United States?

- Atlantic (Ocean)

Explanation: The United States is bordered on the East by the Atlantic Ocean. This ocean extends from the American East coast to Europe and Africa. Another interesting fact is that the initial 13 colonies had been founded along the coast of the Atlantic Ocean.

91. Name one U.S. territory.

- Puerto Rico

- U.S. Virgin Islands

- American Samoa

- Northern Mariana Islands

- Guam

Explanation: The "U.S. territories" are territories located between the Pacific Ocean and the Caribbean Sea that, while not part of the American continent, are under the jurisdiction of the U.S. government.

92. Name one state that borders Canada.

- Maine
- New Hampshire
- Vermont
- New York
- Pennsylvania
- Ohio
- Michigan
- Minnesota
- North Dakota
- Montana
- Idaho
- Washington
- Alaska

93. Name one state that borders Mexico.

- California

- Arizona

- New Mexico

- Texas

94. What is the capital of the United States? *

- Washington, D.C.

95. Where is the Statue of Liberty? *

- New York (Harbor)

- Liberty Island

[Also acceptable are New Jersey, near New York City, and on the Hudson River.]

Explanation: In 1886, the people of France gave a gift of friendship to the U.S. in the form of a copper statue that is called "The statue of Liberty," installed at Liberty Island on the Hudson River in New York City (harbor).

Symbols

96. Why does the flag have 13 stripes?

- Because there were 13 original colonies

- Because the stripes represent the original colonies

Explanation: Same explanation as question 97

97. Why does the flag have 50 stars? *

- Because there is one star for each state

- Because each star represents a state

- Because there are 50 states

Explanation: The American flag has 13 stripes and 50 stars. The stripes symbolize the former 13 colonies, whereas the stars symbolize the current 50 American states. Each star represents a state, and there is one star for every state. (Same explanation for question: 96)

98. What is the name of the national anthem?

- The Star-Spangled Banner

Explanation: The national anthem is called "The Star-Spangled Banner." The anthem revolves around the American flag. During the War of 1812, British ships stormed Fort McHenry in Baltimore one night. Throughout the night, bombs burst. From a ship, an American named Francis Scott Key saw the battle. He was concerned that the U.S. would lose the fight. The next day, he noticed the American flag flapping in the breeze. He was aware that the United States had won the fight. Then he composed "The Star-Spangled Banner," which is currently the United States national anthem.

Holidays

99. When do we celebrate Independence Day? *

- July 4

Explanation: The thirteen former colonies of the U.S. declared independence from the British Empire through the Declaration of Independence on July 4, 1776. July 4th has been ever since celebrated as a national holiday each year to commemorate the Independence Day of the country.

100. Name <u>two</u> national U.S. holidays.

- New Year's Day
- Martin Luther King, Jr. Day
- Presidents' Day
- Memorial Day
- Independence Day
- Labor Day

- Columbus Day
- Veterans Day
- Thanksgiving
- Juneteenth
- Christmas

Civics practice test

In this chapter, you will find 8 sets of questions randomly drawn from the pool of 100 official USCIS questions.

Each set will consist of 10 questions, since 10 is the maximum number of questions you can be asked during the civics test.

Remember that during the real test, these questions will be asked verbally, and you will have to answer them verbally.

Remember also you will only need to answer 6 questions correctly to pass this part of the naturalization exam.

Civics practice test 1 – questions

1.
Who is the Commander-in-Chief of the military?

_____

2.
During the Cold War, what was the main concern of the United States?

_____

3.
Who did the United States fight in World War II?

_____

4.
What are the two parts of the U.S. Congress?

_____

5.

What does the Constitution do?

_____

6.

We elect a President for how many years?

_____

7.

What movement tried to end racial discrimination?

_____

8.

How old do citizens have to be to vote for President? *

_____

9.

What is the highest court in the United States?

_____

10.

What was <u>one</u> important thing that Abraham Lincoln did?

_____

Civics practice test 1 – answers

Question 1

- The President

Question 2

- Communism

Question 3

- Japan, Germany, and Italy

Question 4

- The Senate and House (of Representatives)

Question 5

- Sets up the government
- Defines the government
- Protects basic rights of Americans

Question 6

- Four (4)

Question 7

- Civil rights (movement)

Question 8

- Eighteen (18) and older

Question 9

- The Supreme Court

Question 10

- Freed the slaves (Emancipation Proclamation)
- Saved (or preserved) the Union
- Led the United States during the Civil War

Civics practice test 2 – questions

1.
What do we show loyalty to when we say the Pledge of Allegiance?

_____

2.
What is <u>one</u> responsibility that is only for United States citizens? *

_____

3.
What is the highest court in the United States?

_____

4.
Who signs bills to become law?

_____

5.
What is <u>one</u> responsibility that is only for United States citizens?

_____

6.
What ocean is on the West Coast of the United States?

_____

7.
Name <u>one</u> state that borders Canada.

_____

8.

Before he was President, Eisenhower was a general. What war was he in?

_____

9.

What are <u>two</u> ways that Americans can participate in their democracy?

_____

10.

What is <u>one</u> reason colonists came to America?

_____

Civics practice test 2 – answers

Question 1

- The United States
- The flag

Question 2

- Serve on a jury
- Vote in a federal election

Question 3

- The Supreme Court

Question 4

- The President

Question 5

- Serve on a jury
- Vote in a federal election

Question 6

- Pacific (Ocean)

Question 7

- Maine
- Minnesota
- New Hampshire
- North Dakota
- Vermont
- Montana
- New York
- Idaho
- Pennsylvania
- Washington
- Ohio
- Alaska
- Michigan

Question 8

- World War II

Question 9

- Vote
- Join a political party
- Help with a campaign
- Join a civic group
- Join a community group
- Give an elected official your opinion on an issue

- Call Senators and Representatives
- Publicly support or oppose an issue or policy
- Run for office
- Write to a newspaper

Question 10

- Freedom
- Political liberty
- Religious freedom

- Economic opportunity
- Practice their religion
- Escape persecution

Civics practice test 3 – questions

1.

The idea of self-government is in the first three words of the Constitution. What are these words?

_____

2.

What are <u>two</u> Cabinet-level positions?

_____

3.

We elect a U.S. Representative for how many years?

_____

4.

If both the President and the Vice President can no longer serve, who becomes President?

_____

5.

Who wrote the Declaration of Independence?

_____

6.

Name <u>one</u> right only for United States citizens.

_____

7.

Who was President during the Great Depression and World War II?

_____

8.

When was the Declaration of Independence adopted?

_____

9.

Who was the first President?

_____

10.

What is the political party of the President now?

_____

Civics practice test 3 – answers

Question 1

- We the People

Question 2

- Secretary of Agriculture
- Secretary of Commerce
- Secretary of Defense
- Secretary of Education
- Secretary of Energy
- Secretary of Health and Human Services
- Secretary of Homeland Security
- Secretary of Housing and Urban Development

- Secretary of the Interior
- Secretary of Labor
- Secretary of State
- Secretary of Transportation
- Secretary of the Treasury
- Secretary of Veterans Affairs
- Attorney General
- Vice President

Question 3

- Two (2)

Question 4

- The Speaker of the House

Question 5

- (Thomas) Jefferson

Question 6

- Vote in a federal election

- Run for federal office

Question 7

- (Franklin) Roosevelt

Question 8

- July 4, 1776

Question 9

- (George) Washington

Question 10

- Democratic party

Civics practice test 4 – questions

1.

What is an amendment?

_____

2.

Why does the flag have 50 stars?

_____

3.

What is the "rule of law"?

_____

4.

What is <u>one</u> thing Benjamin Franklin is famous for?

_____

5.

How many U.S. Senators are there?

_____

6.

What is the capital of the United States? *

_____

7.

Name <u>one</u> problem that led to the Civil War.

_____

8.

What ocean is on the East Coast of the United States?

_____

9.

What group of people was taken to America and sold as slaves?

_____

10.

Who is the "Father of Our Country"?

_____

Civics practice test 4 – answers

Question 1

- A change (to the Constitution)
- An addition (to the Constitution)

Question 2

- Because there is one star for each state
- Because each star represents a state
- Because there are 50 states

Question 3

- Everyone must follow the law
- Leaders must obey the law
- Government must obey the law
- No one is above the law

Question 4

- U.S. diplomat
- Oldest member of the Constitutional Convention
- First Postmaster General of the United States
- Writer of "Poor Richard's Almanac"
- Started the first free libraries

Question 5

- One hundred (100)

Question 6

- Washington, D.C.

Question 7

- Slavery

- Economic reasons

- States' rights

Question 8

- Atlantic (Ocean)

Question 9

- Africans

- People from Africa

Question 10

- (George) Washington

Civics practice test 5 – questions

1.
What did Martin Luther King, Jr. do?

_____

2.
If the President can no longer serve, who becomes President?

_____

3.
Name <u>one</u> U.S. territory.

_____

4.
Who vetoes bills?

_____

5.
What is the economic system in the United States?

_____

6.
Who does a U.S. Senator represent?

_____

7.
Where is the Statue of Liberty?

_____

8.

Name <u>one</u> American Indian tribe in the United States.

9.

In what month do we vote for President?

10.

What is freedom of religion?

Civics practice test 5 – answers

Question 1

- Fought for civil rights

- Worked for equality for all Americans

Question 2

- The Vice President

Question 3

- Puerto Rico

- U.S. Virgin Islands

- American Samoa

- Northern Mariana Islands

- Guam

Question 4

- The President

Question 5

- Capitalist economy

- Market economy

Question 6

- All people of the state

Question 7

- New York (Harbor)

- Liberty Island

Question 8

- Cherokee
- Navajo
- Sioux
- Chippewa
- Choctaw
- Pueblo
- Apache
- Iroquois
- Creek
- Blackfeet
- Seminole
- Cheyenne
- Arawak
- Shawnee
- Mohegan
- Huron
- Oneida
- Lakota
- Crow
- Teton
- Hopi
- Inuit

Question 9

- November

Question 10

- You can practice any religion, or not practice a religion

Civics practice test 6 – questions

1.

What major event happened on September 11, 2001, in the United States?

_____

2.

In what month do we vote for President?

_____

3.

Name <u>one</u> state that borders Mexico.

_____

4.

Why does the flag have 13 stripes?

_____

5.

What is the name of the President of the United States now?

_____

6.

How many justices are on the Supreme Court?

_____

7.

What did the Emancipation Proclamation do?

_____

8.

What does the President's Cabinet do?

_____

9.

There were 13 original states. Name <u>three</u>.

_____

10.

We elect a U.S. Senator for how many years?

Civics practice test 6 – answers

Question 1

- Terrorists attacked the United States

Question 2

- November

Question 3

- California

- Arizona

- New Mexico

- Texas

Question 4

- Because there were 13 original colonies

- Because the stripes represent the original colonies

Question 5

- Joe Biden

Question 6

- Nine

Question 7

- Freed the slaves

- Freed slaves in the Confederacy

- Freed slaves in the Confederate states

- Freed slaves in most Southern states

Question 8

- Advises the President

Question 9

- New Hampshire
- Massachusetts
- Rhode Island
- Connecticut
- New York
- New Jersey
- Pennsylvania

- Delaware
- Maryland
- Virginia
- North Carolina
- South Carolina
- Georgia

Question 10

- Six (6)

Civics practice test 7 – questions

1.

What is the name of the national anthem?

_____

2.

Who lived in America before the Europeans arrived?

_____

3.

The Federalist Papers supported the passage of the U.S. Constitution. Name <u>one</u> of the writers.

_____

4.

What is the supreme law of the land?

_____

5.

When is the last day you can send in federal income tax forms?

_____

6.

What does the judicial branch do?

_____

7.

What are <u>two</u> rights of everyone living in the United States?

_____

8.

The House of Representatives has how many voting members?

_____

9.

Who is the Chief Justice of the United States now?

_____

10.

What is <u>one</u> promise you make when you become a United States citizen?

_____

Civics practice test 7 – answers

Question 1

- The Star-Spangled Banner

Question 2

- American Indians

- Native Americans

Question 3

- (James) Madison

- (Alexander) Hamilton

- (John) Jay

- Publius

Question 4

- The Constitution

Question 5

- April 15

Question 6

- Reviews laws

- Explains laws

- Resolves disputes (disagreements)

- Decides if a law goes against the Constitution

Question 7

- Freedom of expression
- Freedom of speech
- Freedom of assembly
- Freedom to petition the government
- Freedom of religion
- The right to bear arms

Question 8

- Four hundred thirty-five (435)

Question 9

- John G. Roberts

Question 10

- Give up loyalty to other countries
- Defend the Constitution and laws of the United States
- Obey the laws of the United States
- Serve in the U.S. military (if needed)
- Serve (do important work for) the nation (if needed)
- Be loyal to the United States

Civics practice test 8 – questions

1.
What did Susan B. Anthony do?

2.
When do we celebrate Independence Day?

3.
How many amendments does the Constitution have?

4.
Why do some states have more Representatives than other states?

5.
Name two national U.S. holidays.

6.
Name one of the two longest rivers in the United States.

7.
Who makes federal laws?

8.

Under our Constitution, some powers belong to the federal government. What is <u>one</u> power of the federal government?

_____

9.

What territory did the United States buy from France in 1803?

_____

10.

What do we call the first ten amendments to the Constitution?

_____

Civics practice test 8 – answers

Question 1

- Fought for women's rights
- Fought for civil rights

Question 2

- July 4

Question 3

- Twenty-seven (27)

Question 4

- (because of) the state's population
- (because) they have more people
- (because) some states have more people

Question 5

- New Year's Day
- Martin Luther King, Jr. Day
- Presidents' Day
- Memorial Day
- Independence Day
- Labor Day
- Columbus Day
- Veterans Day
- Thanksgiving
- Christmas

Question 6

- Missouri (River)
- Mississippi (River)

Question 7

- Congress

- Senate and House (of Representatives)

- (U.S. or national) legislature

Question 8

- To print money

- To declare war

- To create an army

- To make treaties

Question 9

- The Louisiana Territory

- Louisiana

Question 10

- The Bill of Rights

Test-Taking Strategies

The most important strategy is to read this guide thoroughly and understand the structure of the test. You will only be able to prepare for the test if you have basic knowledge of it. Some strategies will be shared below, which will help you in preparation for your naturalization test.

Follow the Study Material

In this guide, every important detail of the test has been provided. Follow each chapter carefully. You have also been provided with practice tests and study material that you need for preparation.

Improve Your English

Half of the test comprises the English portion. You need to have a basic level of English proficiency for this test. You can improve your English by watching your favorite English series. By reading the subtitles, you can also improve your reading skills. For speaking, try practicing English with your friends and family.

Take Practice Tests

Practice is a key tool of learning. Take advantage of the practice tests in this guide to get as much practice as possible.

Learn Civics Portion in Parts

In chapter 3, you have been provided with the civics portion in a story format. Try learning the civics portion by dividing it into small portions as we have already done for you, and if you have enough time, learn each section in a day.

Stay Updated

The civics portion has many questions that are related to current affairs. You can easily learn the names of the President, Vice President, Senator, etc., if you actively listen and watch the news. It will also help you in the English section.

Top Reasons for Application Denial and Strategies to Avoid Them

Taking U.S. citizenship is a long and quite expensive process. You will not like to make any mistake that can become the reason for your application failure. The major reasons that will be discussed in the section below, which can become the cause of your application denial.

Failing Civics test

Failing the civics test can result in the denial of your application, therefore do not take it for granted.

Failing English Test

As mentioned, you must pass all three sections of the English test, i.e., reading, writing, and speaking. Failing one or all twice can fail your citizenship application.

Failing to Understand or Speak English During the Interview

Your Interview will be taken in English. You will not be allowed to have an interpreter, and the Interview will be conducted in English. Failing to understand or speak English during the N-400 application process can fail your application. The officer will ask you simple questions related to your application to test your English-speaking ability.

Filing Too Early

We have provided you with all the information and residency requirements that must be met before applying for U.S. citizenship. If you are still unsure of when to apply, you can use the calculator you find by scanning this QR code:

This will help you calculate your residence requirement and let you know if you are eligible for naturalization. You can submit the application 90 calendar days before completing the permanent resident requirement. However, our suggestion is to submit your application a couple of days after the earliest effective date, as in the past some applications submitted on the earliest effective date have been rejected due to errors by the offices in calculating timelines.

Missing Your Interview

You will be sent a mail a month before your interview date. Sometimes because of a delay from the postal service, you can miss your Interview. Therefore, you need to have an online account from where you can check your application status and the date of your Interview. Check the document tab on your account regularly. Your letter will be displayed on this tab. Do not miss your Interview under any circumstances. However, if an unfortunate incident occurs and you miss your Interview, call USCIS at your earliest convenience and try to reschedule a new interview by stating your reason for missing the Interview.

Changing Your Marital Status During the Process

If you are applying through marriage, by the time you are processing your naturalization application, you must be living with your U.S. citizen spouse until the oath ceremony. If you separate or divorce during the process, you will no longer be eligible to apply through marriage, and your application will be denied. You will then need to withdraw your application and apply under the five-year eligibility later.

Not Meeting the Physical Presence Requirement

You can travel during the process of your N-400 application. However, you will need to be physically present during the interviews and complete your residence requirement as well. You must also be present for half of the time during your statutory period in the United States.

Not Meeting the Continuous Residence Requirement

The amount of time needed to meet continuous residency requirements was discussed in detail in Chapter 2. If you fail to meet the continuous residence requirement, your application will be denied. Extended absence from the U.S. can disrupt your continuous residence; therefore, you should try to avoid it. A trip of fewer than 6 months outside the U.S. will not disrupt your continuous residence and vice-versa.

If, for any emergency, you had to leave the U.S. for more than 6 years, you will have to provide proof of your absence to the officer to prove that despite your absence, you continued to have a connection with the United States. You can submit the following documents to prove your connections to the US:

- Tax return transcripts

- Proof of not working in any other country

- Proof of residence of immediate family in the U.S. during your absence

- Proof of your job in the US

- Proof of car registration and insurance

- Mortgage payment receipts

- Utility payments receipts

Not Registering for the Selective Service

As mentioned, you will need to register for the selective service and should be ready to voluntarily serve the country when needed. If you do not register for the selective service, this will result in the denial of your application. Note: this only applies to male applicants.

Lack of Good Moral Character

"An applicant for naturalization must show that he or she has been and continues to be a person of good moral character." -USCIS

This applies to both the five-year period when you apply for naturalization and also the period before that.

The following acts come under a lack of good moral character:

- Habitual drinking

- Driving under the influence of alcohol/drugs

- Illegal gambling

- Involvement in a crime

If you have been a former criminal or have a police record, consult an immigration attorney.

Failing to File Taxes

It also shows that you have a good moral character. Try to file your taxes timely to avoid any issues during your naturalization process.

Failing to Pay Child Support/Alimony

You must pay your child support or alimony in a timely manner if you have any. Keep your documents clear and present during the time of the Interview.

Failing to Submit Documents Timely

If you are asked to bring additional documents after your Interview, try to submit them as soon as possible to avoid further problems.

Lying on Your Application and/or Interview

You are under oath during your Interview. Do not lie about anything. If you have any doubts, you can always ask the officer.

Top 7 Mistakes to Avoid at Your Interviews

1. Failing to Review Your N-400 Application Form

As discussed above, the designated officer will ask you questions from your application form. Simply put, your answers must be consistent with the answers you have provided in your application form. You have already been warned that you should never lie on your application form or during your Interview. If for any reason you fail to provide consistent answers to your application during your Interview, it will make you look suspicious and might result in the decline of your application. Therefore, try to revise your application before going for the Interview.

2. Not Remembering the Changes Made to Your Application

If you have made any changes to your application based on new information, for example a new postal address, etc., try to make a list of all these changes so that you can avoid any suspicion during your Interview.

3. Forgetting Your Original Documents on the Day of the Interview

During the Interview, applicants should submit all documents necessary to support what they stated during the application.

In particular, we recommend that you always carry with you (The following list is provided by the U.S. Citizen and Immigration Service):

- Your interview appointment notice.

- Form I-551, Permanent Resident Card.

- A state-issued identification, such as a driver's license.

- All valid and expired passports and travel documents issued to you that document your absences from the United States since becoming a permanent resident.

- For a list of other documents that you may need to bring with you, read Form M-477, Document Checklist.

If you fail to present these documents, it will result in a negative impression on the officer and, in the worst case, may lead to the rejection of your application.

4. <u>Arriving Late for Your Interview</u>

As mentioned in the previous chapter, if you encounter any emergency, immediately contact USCIS and inform them of your situation. They will either reschedule your Interview or accommodate you at a later time on the same day if you are late by a few minutes or less than an hour. However, you should not be late as this will make a bad impression and can hinder your naturalization process.

5. <u>Guessing the Answers</u>

If English is not your first language and you have difficulty understanding the question, ask the officer to explain the question to you in more detail or in simple language. However, if you try guessing the answer, it will result in building suspicion around your case, and the officer will start deeply analyzing your case. Worse, your application can be denied.

6. <u>Inappropriate Dressing</u>

Try to dress in formal dress on the day of the Interview. Avoid wearing the following:

- Jeans

- Shorts

- Sweatpants

- Pants

- Tank tops

- Flip flops

- T-shirts with inappropriate printings, such as religious or political slogans or offensive graphics

Wear a comfortable dress on the day of the Interview.

7. <u>Failing to Study for the English and Civics Tests</u>

A major portion of this guide has been dedicated to the study and practice of English and civics tests.

This is because these are very important and will eventually decide your eligibility for naturalization.

Therefore, focus on these areas and study the material that has been provided in this guide.

How To Fix Mistakes In N-400 Application

If you accidentally commit a mistake in your N-400, you can amend these mistakes. First, you must take care during the writing and submission process of your application. When you complete filling out your application, before submitting it:

- Review your application twice or three times to make sure you have written everything correctly.

- Review your application with a friend or family member.

- Make a copy of your application before posting it or submitting it online so that you can read it after and amend any possible mistakes.

If even after following these steps you make a mistake, do the following:

- Write down all the errors that you have made.

- Gather supporting documents to support any changes that you wish to make or that you have accidentally entered wrong during the application process.

- Bring the supporting documents on the day of your Interview and notify the officer of the errors that you have accidentally made.

What Can Disqualify You from U.S. Citizenship?

If you:

- Voluntarily give up your U.S. Citizenship, you will automatically be disqualified for U.S. citizenship.

- Join the armed forces of a foreign country.

- Run for public office in a foreign country.

- Commit an act of treason against the United States.

Timeline Description of Your Application Process

The average processing type for becoming a U.S. citizen is around 14.5 months. This is only the application process, and the overall naturalization process will take more time, as it involves other steps as well. The total time for Naturalization ranges from 18.5 to 24 months. It is completed in the following 5 steps:

- The N-400 Application process takes around 14.5 months.

- Biometric appointment attendance. This is the formal process of taking your fingerprints, and it is scheduled about a month after USCIS receives your citizenship application.

- Attending your citizenship interview takes around 14 months. This step involves English and civics tests.

- You will receive a decision in writing of either approval or continuation of your application within 120 days of your test. Your application will be continued if you do not pass the tests or if you fail to produce all the required documents at the time of the Interview. Your application can also be denied if you fail the test twice, or if you commit any mistake that has been mentioned in the previous section.

- If the application is approved, it is likely that the oath ceremony will be held on the same day as the interview and you will receive your citizenship certificate at the end of the ceremony. If not, you will receive a letter with the date and location of the next ceremony you can attend, which usually takes place between 2 and 6 weeks after the exam. Even then you will receive your certificate at the end of the oath ceremony. Remember, even after you complete all the steps, the oath is necessary, and you must show up for your oath on the scheduled date. Failing it will result in the non-issuance of your Naturalization Certificate.

Dear Future American Citizen,

first of all, thank you again for purchasing our product.

Secondly, congratulations! If you are using our Guide, you are among those few who are willing to do whatever it takes to excel on the exam and are not satisfied with just trying.

We create our Study Guides in the same spirit. We want to offer our students only the best to help them get only the best through precise, accurate, and easy-to-use information.

That is why **your success is our success**, and if you think our Guide helped you achieve your goals, we would love it if you could take 60 seconds of your time to leave us a review on Amazon.

Thank you again for trusting us by choosing our Guide, and good luck with your new life as a U.S. citizen.

Sincerely,
H.S. Test Preparation Team

Scan the QR code to leave a review (it only takes you 60 seconds):

References

1.
Constitution, U.S. (1787)
2.
Constitution, U.S. (1791). First Amendment
3.
Schwartz, B. (1992). *The great rights of mankind: A history of the American 4.*
4.
Bill of Rights. Rowman & Littlefield.
5.
Chapter 2 – *English and Civics testing.* USCIS. (2021).
6.
Volume 12 -*Citizenship and Naturalization.* USCIS. (2021).
7.
How the exam works
https://www.immigrationfamilylawyer.com/
Law office of Van T. Doan
7.1
https://www.aparicioimmigrationlaw.com/
Aparicio immigration law
7.2
Guidance on Naturalization Civics Educational Requirement
file:///C:/Users/alber/Downloads/21022232-2.pdf
U.S. Citizen and Immigration Service
8.
Information on the Civics test 2020
https://www.uscis.gov/citizenship/2020test
U.S. Citizen and Immigration Service
9.
Information on how the U.S. government works
https://constitutionus.com/us-naturalization-test/if-President-and-vice-President-cannot-serve-who-becomes-President/
https://constitutionus.com/us-naturalization-test/what-does-Presidents-cabinet-do/
Constitutionus
https://en.wikipedia.org/wiki/Constitution_of_the_United_States
Wikipedia
10.
Information on the civil war
https://en.wikipedia.org/wiki/American_Civil_War_Centennial
Wikipedia
11.
Quotes from the U.S. Constitution
https://uscode.house.gov/static/constitution.pdf
Archives of the U.S. House of Representatives
12.
Quotes from the Declaration of Independence
https://www.archives.gov/founding-docs/declaration-transcript
U.S. National Archives
13.
Information on what documents to bring to the interview
https://my.uscis.gov/citizenship/what_to_expect
U.S. Citizen and Immigration Service

Credits

1.
Cover:
this cover has been designed using assets from Freepik.com.
Item 1 URL: https://www.freepik.com/free-photo/low-angle-shot-amazing-statue-liberty-new-york-usa_13562105.htm
Item 2 URL: https://www.freepik.com/free-photo/american-flag-isolated-white_20989005.htm#query=isolated%20us%20white&position=1&from_view=keyword
Both items are subject to a free license that allows use of the content for commercial and personal projects, on digital or printed media, for an unlimited number of times and without any time limits, from anywhere in the world, to make modifications and create derivative works.
2.
Civics Test Questions
All 100 civics test questions were taken from the official USCIS website
https://www.uscis.gov/sites/default/files/document/questions-and-answers/100q.pdf
3.
Explanations of procedures and timelines
Explanations regarding examination procedures and timelines faithfully reproduce what is reported in this regard on the official USCIS website.
https://www.uscis.gov/
4.
Writing Vocabulary List
The Writing Vocabulary List image is from the official USCIS website
https://www.uscis.gov/sites/default/files/document/guides/writing_vocab.pdf
5.
Reading Vocabulary List
The Reading Vocabulary List image is from the official USCIS website
https://www.uscis.gov/sites/default/files/document/guides/reading_vocab.pdf

Made in the USA
Las Vegas, NV
28 November 2024